Anita -

Let the
Sun Shine In

Blessings of
Love
and Light,

With love,
Lin & Ed

Lin Brian

ISBN-13: 978-1983579790
ISBN-10:1983579793

Easytime Publishing

Lake Havasu City, AZ
www.EasytimePublishing.com
easytime@me.com

TABLE OF CONTENTS

ACKNOWLEDGMENTS

How can I possibly thank everyone who has contributed their support in getting this second book published? Where do I start?

My husband, Ed, continues to teach me more about myself than I thought possible. He is the glue that holds me together when I come unglued.

To my late mother, Pearl Tammie, who always believed in me, thank you for being my mom.

To my children, Tami-Lin Graham, Daina Brian and Ritchie Brian, thank you for teaching me valuable lessons about being a mother and letting go.

To Maureen Sparrow, who read poems out loud to me, so I could hear the cadence, thank you.

To Francine Stringer, who bought a book, then called and asked if I would please mail copies to two of her friends in Vancouver, BC., thank you.

To Brian Holmberg, a childhood friend, and his partner, Ellie, who bought one book, then immediately phoned and ordered ten more, thank you.

And to those who have said, "I want a copy of whatever you write," yet another thank you.

To everyone who believes in my writing, you have given me the courage to publish. Thank you, BJ Alexander, Gail Prior, Linda Cipolla, Louise Lapierre, Marie Tallon, Monique Gerbasi, Noreen Dorais, Pat Armishaw, Pat Lane, Sheree Mann, and Ursula Wick. You have all given me gems of wisdom that oft times translate into poems. Being there for each other is one of the greatest gifts I know.

My Publisher, Paul Bailey, of Easytime Publishing, has unscrambled the path to publishing for me. He has also honoured me by asking me to write two poems. They bracket his recently published book, "The Rich Boys". Both my previous book, "Out of Darkness Into Light" and Paul's "The Rich Boys" are available on Paul's website, http://www.easytimepublishing.com/

vii

FORWARD

In Lin Brian's first book, "Out of Darkness Into Light" she led the reader out of the hurts, abuses, and traumas of life and into the hope of new light.

In this, her second book, Lin highlights new ways of thinking. She reminds us to be aware of our responsibility to focus on happiness. Life is meant to be joyful, but we often get in our own way. "Let the Sun Shine In" brings awareness. By cultivating that awareness, we can change and feel the sun more often.

"Let the Sun Shine In" is a compilation of poems written over 30 years.

Blessed Be.

PRAYER

What am I on earth for?
Is there something I can teach?
And *if* I find the answer,
how many can I reach?
How many are not valued?
And are misunderstood?
How many have the feeling
they simply are no good?
Oh, I need to tell them all,
"This clearly is not true.
Each of you deserves the best,
just because you're you!"

OUR CANDLES

Light a candle.
Dispel the gloom
of winter's darkness,
and make room
for feeling summer's glorious light,
filling us with pure delight.

WRITING

I am a writer, honest, true.
The words I write, from me to you
sometimes sparkle in the air,
like diamonds precious in my hair.
Sometimes writing makes me blue,
but – still a gift I share with you.

Like carrot dangling on a string,
I never know what it will bring.
Sometimes sorrow – at others, pleasure,
bringing joy I cannot measure.
As ripened fruit delights the taste,
to not be writing would be a waste.

WISDOM WORDS

Sometimes at night these wisdom words
start rolling through my head.
You know, the time we're most relaxed
once we go to bed.
When I awake in morning,
the words so clear before
that I didn't think I had to write
are gone forevermore.
I think it is a lesson
to capture words with pen,
so when I want to **do** the poem,
I can find the words again.

FUN

Sitting in the sun
is fun.
In the rain,
it's fun again.
Really, truly, don't you find
that fun is just a state of mind?

US

I smile inside when I'm with you.
What the heck's a girl to do?
Can't get enough... of loving you.

My heart expands, my legs get weak,
and sometimes I can hardly speak.
I catch myself lost in dreams,
reliving love we've shared. It seems
as if I think of nothing else
except your love, your face, your smile.
And all I really want in life
is to feel these feelings for awhile.

I give myself the gift of you,
of who you are and what you do.
I've learned to love and learned to take
what's offered me. Make no mistake.
The love you give I will return,
as deep inside the fires burn.
I will take and give, and give and take,
in hopes that we will always make
the magic of our love come true,
and always feel like this, we two.

I WONDER

Sometimes I wonder if I know you at all.
As each new experience between us takes place,
I see a new you, one I had not seen before,
and the depth of my feelings surprises me.
I wonder if I will ever get to know you,
or if I even want to,
or if I'd rather the poignancy of learning you
to go on and on throughout the rest of our lives,
giving new meaning to our love
and our commitment to each other.

Each day is a new beginning,
and I get a chance to glimpse
a little more of who you are,
and rejoice in that newfound knowledge.

Perhaps we are just getting
more comfortable with each other
as we move into a new chapter
and dedicate more time
to doing things we want.

I look forward to the rest of our lives.

THE LOVE I FEEL FOR YOU

I know a love that's strong and true.
This is the love I feel for you.
Much different than the love that was.
Strangely true. Is this because
you treat me in a different way?
You now can hear just what I say?

Our words are now more understood,
and that makes both of us feel good.
Today we are so much more real.
We speak the very way we feel.
We find it works, and know we must.
It is the way to build the trust.

WHY ... I ... LOVE ... YOU

While I don't always thank you for the thoughtful things you do,
they are one of many reasons why ... I ... LOVE ... YOU.

Your wit, your sense of humour, your intelligence, your charm.
When we're walking out together, it's how you take my arm.

How you put your arms around me when I'm feeling so uptight.
I don't know how, but somehow, things feel more alright.

It's in your creativity, the delicious meals you cook.
For a more appreciative taster, you don't have to look.

It's in how you attend our every need, providing wine and food,
as I visit with a friend of mine. Makes both of us feel good.

These only scratch the surface of the many things you do,
as I attempt to tell you why ... I ... LOVE ... YOU.

MY GIRLFRIEND

Beautiful hair and eyes of brown.
On your head I see a crown
of flowers dressed in every hue.
This is how my heart sees you.
It fairly sings, your vibrant spirit.
It lights my life. Can you hear it?
Philosophical and craving knowledge.
We both know you'll go to college.

In tune with art and picture taking,
I see someone famous in the making.
You look at things, just 'cuz they are,
and in my eyes, you are a star.
You've shared with me the things you fear,
and that's the trait I hold most dear.
We don't hold back. We get it out.
I love you so! I want to shout.

It's fun to watch you cheer your team.
You really rock. Know what I mean?
Especially the Denver Broncos,
When you're yelling, "Go! Team!! Go!!"
There is strength in you that I admire.
You give so much. You do inspire.
When you believe, you're very strong.
You'll fight for right. Against all wrong.

They say absence makes the heart grow fonder.
Who said that? And why, I wonder.
I couldn't love you any more
than all the time I did before.
When I think of you my world gets hazy
and sometimes others think I'm crazy.
I miss you so when you're away.
More than 'I Love You' I cannot say.
It amazes me, your zest for life.
Someday I hope you'll be my wife.

MY WIFE

From out of nowhere you came and took my hand,
as if we'd always been together, as if it had been planned.
My life, that seemed so dead before, now has come alive.
Instead of feeling wasted, it seems to grow and thrive.

You're a juggernaut of energy, so happy, full of life.
Of all the women in the world, I'm glad you are my wife.
You have a sense of justice that is beautiful and rare,
and hate to see the small guy hurt in life by what's not fair.

While you cannot comprehend places you've not been,
you always try to understand the things that I have seen.
And when my past drags me down, and I'm not always there,
you keep life rolling normally. It shows how much you care.

No matter what my project is, you always lend a hand,
even when it takes away from things that you had planned.
Your honesty's refreshing. Your mind you always speak.
I value that. It bolsters me. False friends I do not seek.

You have your own views of the world, you have your visions true.
You take the time to dream your dreams,
and somehow follow through.
For all the things you are, and for all the things you do,
I know how very blessed I am, to share my life with you.

BABY

A new baby is a special thing.
Into your life much joy she'll bring.
As she learns about life and starts to grow,
Love, pride, and joy, in her you will know.

For never was a girl so smart,
and quick to capture every heart.
And never did one learn so fast
as yours. Observe. Just watch. Just ask.

You must be proud of your new son.
In all the world he is the one
to wrap his hand around your heart,
and give your life a brand new start.

You'll be delighted as he grows.
He'll be the best. The whole world knows
our babies give our heart a lift,
truly one of God's great gifts.

CHILDREN

Children are one of God's most precious gifts,
to have and to hold, to share and to mold.
To watch over and teach until they are grown,
and have some children of their own.

MY CHILDREN

My visit with you, daughter... son,
was oh-so-good and it was fun.
I wish you both peace and all good things
that living in the moment brings.

I regret we live so far apart.
Please know you're always in my heart.
And really, it is not so far –
four hours when we drive by car.

Know that I'll be back again
to spend time with you. It's very plain.
We simply need to make the time.
To not do so would be a crime.

DAUGHTER'S BIRTHDAY

Remember when you were young
and you just couldn't wait
to get a few years older.
Well, now you're thirty-eight.

Like most, you probably notice
the years have gone too fast.
We have memories of good times,
and those will always last.

Every child you have born
is as precious to you as gold,
from the time that you first saw him,
had him in your arms to hold.

Remember all the love you feel
is no different than mine.
The love I feel for my daughter
transcends the sands of time.

SON'S BIRTHDAY

As we look back across the years,
that we have watched you grow,
we are just that much prouder
than you will ever know.

There is so much to tell you,
it's impossible to say
how much joy you're being wished
as you celebrate *your* day!

Our good thoughts will follow you
throughout the coming years,
as you walk into new frontiers,
as you confront your fears.

And we will count our blessings,
celebrate your success.
We always want what's best for you.
Good Luck, our son. God Bless.

MY BROTHER

My brother found, when he awoke,
he was immobilized by stroke.
That was a thought that he had never
thought – it changed his life forever.

No longer can he drive his car,
and he just cannot walk too far.
He would like to have the use
of the arm that's hanging loose.

All kinds of things he must address.
Don't know how, I must confess.
There's too much he's had to bear,
and yet he has good will to spare.

When I think of him, I am amazed.
He so deserves to be praised.
His cheerful smile, his countenance
he offers in abundance.

When I think what he's been through,
it should give me a damn good clue.
Smile more and worry less.
Let go of things that cause me stress.
I can learn from him. Oh Yes!!!

MY MOM

Of all the things we've said before,
of all the things we've done,
the things that we have yet to do,
I'm glad you are the one.
The one who tucked me in at night,
who kept me safe and warm,
who stayed up when I had earaches,
who saved me from the storm.
You have been as good to me
as any mom could be.
One reason out of many
that you mean the world to me.

MOTHER'S DAY

As Mother's Day rolls round again,
I think of days gone by,
of home, and you, and how it was,
and how the time does fly.

When I was young, I didn't think
of worries, troubles, cares.
There was nothing I couldn't do,
for weren't you always there?

To help, to guide, to comfort me
when anything went wrong.
I never questioned your ability.
To me you were so strong.

The years have passed and time has gone.
Now I'm a mother, too.
I realize the strength of love
that sees a mother through.

No matter what a child does,
a mom will understand.
She guides and helps unselfishly,
will always lend a hand.

For all these things, and many more,
much more than I can say.
My heart and love are in this wish.
"Happy Mother's Day!"

AGING

Intentness of a daughter as she bends her head to listen.
And isn't that a teardrop in her eye that I see glisten?
She takes her mother's hand in hers
and remembers days long past, her mother, strong and healthy.
She thought those days would last.

But aging has a crazy way of turning hair to grey.
As we mature, we realize no one's here to stay.
Sadness creeps into her heart for a mother growing old.
In her imagination, there are memories to behold.

The times she rode on mother's lap, comforted to sleep,
as daddy drove the family car. Now there's a memory to keep.
She remembers all the dresses her mother used to sew.
She wore them all so proudly, wherever she would go.

And oh! The meals she tasted, made by her mother's hands.
She took it all for granted. She didn't understand.
This is no dress rehearsal. She's feeling the dismay,
as she realizes life won't always be as it is today.

Our parents, they get older. It's hard to see them change.
Their health, it is declining. Our world now seems strange.
And yes, they used to be the ones who gave us all our care.
and now it is the opposite. We know we must be there,

to advocate for them, see they get just what they need.
It's harder than we ever thought. Oh yes, it is, indeed.
As we traverse unknown paths, we cannot do much more
than take comfort in the caring words of those
who've gone before.

REFLECTIONS

Reflections of a mother's love
is something sent from up above.
What's the legacy I will leave?
Will there be something they will grieve?

I do not wish upon them sorrow.
I wish them hope for each tomorrow.
But what is mostly on my mind,
is trust in them, that they will find

all their answers lie within.
All life's challenges have been
the way to access things they know
but have forgotten... and so

alone, must face each challenge brought
forth to us, until we're taught
what we once knew, but have forgot.
We find the serenity we have sought.

PHONE CALL

Just got a phone call from heaven.
It's mommy. She's doing just fine.
She's with all of her friends who traveled before,
and she's having a wonderful time.

There's daddy, there's Warner, there's Mike and there's Anne,
Ilene and Ralph Ritchers, Big Fred, and Fran.
Close girlfriend Shirley, Alec, Edie and Gwen,
Ethyl and Frank, pleased to see her again.

Three sisters, a brother, a mother and dad
went on before... all the family she had.
They all have such smiles wreathed o'er their face,
as they welcome mommy to this wonderful place.

Bill Lusby, Ole, Sylvia, Billie,
Great Uncle Johnny, the Dodds, Jack and Tillie.
Navy buddy Walter, and his wife, Peggy Bay,
all cheering her on as she walks proudly their way.

With held head up high and eyes that can see,
with ears that can hear, with no pardon me,
no laboured breathing, no wracking cough,
no body parts hurting as she walks this new walk.

She would have left us long ago
to join those up above,
but felt a need to stay down here
with those of us she loved.

She would not want us to worry.
She'd not want not us to grieve.
She'd want us to be kind to each other,
and know it was her time to leave.

And although we miss her,
we know that it is best.
She's not cold and she's not hurting.
Yes. Now she is at rest.

Just got a phone call from heaven.
It's mommy. She's doing just fine.
She's with all of her friends who traveled before,
and she's having a wonderful time.

SHE'S NOT THERE

I pick up my phone to call her,
and realize she is not there.
I know she has gone to a better place
and I cannot visit her there.

Now her birthday is coming.
I can't even give her a kiss,
like on all the birthdays she had before.
These are the things that I miss.

I miss her love and supporting me.
She always believed I'd succeed.
No matter what endeavour I tried,
she'd be the comfort I'd need.

Not everyone can believe in us
the way a mother believes.
Experiencing years and years of her love
Now it's gone. I miss it and grieve.

The unconditional love she gave
to each of her three grateful children.
She worried when we lost our way,
relaxed when we found it again.

And Mother's Day is coming, too
with no mother to honour with gift.
I know she is watching from way up on high,
and that gives my heart a lift.

But how, oh how, do we fill the void
that has been left by her leaving?
How do we go on with our lives
and stop spending our days full of grieving?

She would not want that, this we all know.
She'd tell us to go dry our tears.
Spend time with your friends, get out in the sun.
You know... I had many good years.

DAD

I never really knew my Dad.
He died when I was twenty-two.
Just as my adult life began,
his life on earth was through.

FATHER

A father is a wondrous thing,
more valuable than gold.
As we grow up, it's hard to watch
our father growing old.

Surely daddy is the man
who always understood.
And isn't he the one who
could always see the good?

Growing up, I know I learned
a thing or two at daddy's hands.
He was so very proud of me
when I became a woman.

I know I'll always miss him.
Now he's gone. You see,
I'm so lucky he was mine.
I have his memory.

GRANDKIDS

Carter is our grandson,
A true and real "Mann".
He delights us, yes he does,
As only Carter can.

He works hard with crafts and hockey.
He's a very busy boy.
And we both love to watch him.
He fills our hearts with joy.

Mackenzie is also precious,
an energetic girl,
busy with her skating
where she jumps and twirls and whirls.

We feel so very lucky
to know our sweetheart Mac.
We may well find when we leave,
we'll have a Mac attack.

Okay, this poem is finished.
There is no more for now.
But one last thing we want to say...
We love these two, and how!

NEPHEW

Spencer is our nephew,
a young and charming six.
No matter what the problem is,
he can prescribe a fix.

No matter what our Spencer does,
no matter what he's wishing,
offered gold and frankincense,
he'd turn it down for fishing.

Last year, the one that got away
was big, a seven-twenty.
In six-year-old, that's twenty-seven,
and we all know that's plenty.

Very good at reasoning,
excelled deductive powers.
No pulling wool over his eyes.
He can reason for hours.

Well loved by all who know him,
with fierce imagination,
he constantly asks questions.
No room for stagnation.

Enamored of our Spencer dear,
delightful, cute, with smarts.
He's well behaved, adorable.
Oh yes! He's caught our hearts!

BROTHER-IN-LAW

A gentle man in thought and deed,
helping all when there was need.
With tender soul and lighted eyes.
You loved to sleep under clear, blue skies.

A royal welcome to all who came,
and it can never be the same
without your spirit in our midst.
Know that you are sorely missed.

We know you look down from skies above
and shower many with your love.
In gentleness, you taught us all,
but had to go when you heard the call.

We know that we will meet again.
There'll be no sorrow. There'll be no pain.
Where bodies are whole. We hear and we see.
Oh! What a marvelous day that will be.

AUNT AND UNCLE

My many memories of you,
as seen through childhood eyes,
are filled with lots of smiles,
and also sunny skies.

You have both been special,
though you lived so far away.
Just knowing you were in the world
brightened up my day.

You made our Christmases special,
and exciting, too.
We were always beside ourselves
to open the presents from you.

In everything you said and did,
it was obvious you cared.
I will always have good memories
of the precious time we shared.

And now I see through adult eyes
and it's still the same to me.
I will always wish you happiness,
wherever you may be!

Happy Fiftieth Wedding Anniversary,
Auntie Myrtle and Uncle Gordon.

ALONE I WALK

Alone I walk on somber beach,
with only dog along. No speech.
There is much joy in solitude,
and knowing this brings gratitude.

I thought to be with other men
would make my world alive again.
But no! My dog is my best friend.
Time with him I love to spend.

For it is he, and only he
who **always** loves to be with me,
who never chooses different place
if he can see **only** see my face.

Some have said that dogs can't think.
I disagree. He is my link
to all in life that's straight and true.
I wish the very same for you.

I know I always see him smile,
if he can walk with me awhile.
That's all he wants. He loves me so.
There is no truer love I know.

DOG

Softly my dog lays his head
on my belly,
and his adoration warms me.

MY DOG

I know he really loves me, and I love my little guy.
It feels all warm and cozy when he snuggles by my thigh.
He's a huge joy in my life. He's really a good egg.
At times as I am walking, he hangs close to my leg.

I've heard it said without a dog, our soul remains asleep.
Not all our soul, but some. It's a feeling that I keep.
I've also heard that eyes are the window to the soul.
Right from the start with big brown eyes, my whole heart he stole.

He looks at me adoringly. He loves me through and through.
A love that's unconditional. I know this to be true.
Easy to see this little boy is personality plus,
and what's more, he's easy. He seldom makes a fuss.

Although, when we put off the walk, he's sure to let us know.
He'll stare at us and even bark to say, "It's time to go!"
And then again, when he can see the bottom of his bowl
he whines and barks. "Keep it full." That seems to be his goal.

And then when we get company, he creates such noise.
He gives excited welcomes, and loses all his poise.
After a minute or two of this, he settles down
and dozes off. We don't even know he is around.

Seems earlier and earlier now, once he has been fed,
he looks at me as if to say, "It's time for bed!
And don't forget my cookies. I want them every night."
Those of us who have a dog know they are quite bright.

They have a language all their own that lets us know
their wants and needs without a word. It's true. Yes, it is so.
I'd give up a lot of things, but never him, my friend.
It's a love so very beautiful that never has an end.

WHAT DOES HE SMELL?

What does he smell,
his nose to the ground?
What is it he sees,
and what has he found?

So intent is he staring
as his nose goes sniff, sniff.
Of what creature, I wonder
does he get a whiff?

All attention, he watches
when we mention walk.
Although he can't speak,
he surely can talk.

He jumps and he wiggles
as he stares at our eyes.
Now we can't change our mind.
It wouldn't be nice.

And when he's not sniffing,
he prances along,
like a Nipissing Stallion.
My heart bursts in song.

To witness this glory,
our gift is his pleasure.
His enjoyment of walking
brings me joy beyond measure.

Just a wee little doggy,
he doesn't ask much,
just a walk, food and water,
some play... and our touch.

BEAUTY OF FRIENDSHIP

What is this thing called friendship?
Where does it get it's start?
Do we know a friend when first we meet?
Does it begin within the heart?

How can we nurture friendship?
This is what we need to know.
We must spend time together
to watch our friendship grow.

There are casual friends, and shopping friends,
and some to take to dinner.
There are friends to share a cup of tea,
and every one a winner.

There are friends with whom I can share
my secrets dark and deep.
The ones who hear with caring ear
are the ones I want to keep.

No matter what I'm feeling,
a friend tries to understand.
Does **not** judge or condemn me,
just lends a helping hand.

She doesn't wait for me to call.
She knows unerringly
when to push me forward,
and when to let me be.

Her very open honesty,
the internal thoughts she shares,
gives me the same permission,
shows me that she cares.

There are some, and we've all met them,
our energies deplete.
After spending time with them,
we always feel quite beat.

Yet others, we are drawn to them.
And this is how we tell –
when we spend time together
they have filled up our well.

I know the things I share with her,
she will not repeat.
She keeps my business to herself,
and so I'm free to speak.

She never treats me differently
than she did the day before,
no matter what is going on.
And who could ask for more?

A BETTER PLACE

When you were born the horns were blown
from near and far, for it was known
the person you would grow to be.
And it is so. We all agree.

This old world's a better place,
for those who know your calming face,
for those who feel the warmth of you,
and feel your love. And Yes! It's true.

Your friendship is indeed a treasure
that brings us many hours of pleasure,
and for which we're grateful, too.
This is the gift we get from you.

SPECIAL

When we meet that special person
we want to call a friend,
the impact that they have on us
is with us to the end.

And although there will be times
in life when we must part,
that special person we call friend
lives within our heart.

CONNECTION

I think about the day we met.
It's a day I won't forget.
I knew. I knew with just a glance,
it wasn't simple happenstance.

No. It was this thing called fate,
and isn't it just oh so great,
to make so quick a deep connection,
for one another feel affection.

Friendship was born, strong and true,
and since day one our friendship grew
into what it is today,
a gift, for sure. That's what I say.

We've played, we've laughed, we've cried together.
We've shared, we've cared, no matter whether
life is good or life is bad,
if we're happy, if we're sad.

Great comfort to know if I need you,
you would come to me, know what to do
to ease my heart and ease my sorrow
and I would have a better tomorrow.

And you know the reverse is true.
If you need me, I will come to you,
to help you laugh or help you cry.
I'd walk, I'd crawl, I'd even fly.

For trouble shared is cut in two.
That is what true friendships do.
You are grandma, sister, friend and mother,
and none of us would choose another.

When I think of you, I see your face.
It glows with love, beauty, grace.
To find a friend like you is rare.
You're not afraid to show you care.

We'll grow old together, you and me,
with more good times in store. You'll see.

HONOUR

I would like to thank you,
but no words can express
my thank-you for this party,
except perhaps, "God Bless!"

We all know, each of us,
planning this took work.
Apparently that's not something
you would ever shirk.

With fatigue and so much company,
what is it that I find?
You were going to do this.
It never left your mind.

You've put this together.
It makes me truly see
your friendship is a blessing.
And you have honoured me.

ESSENCE

I am unsure that this poem will do.
Will it capture the full essence of you?
Those of us seekers are sure to know
the energy you emit. It really does show.

There are many, I'm sure, who **do** see your light,
who bask in your presence, in pure delight.
You and I know. It makes perfect sense.
In life, when we meet, there are no accidents.

We find we meet those who fill up our well,
who shore up the body within which we dwell.
Who shore up our psyche and help heal our spirit.
Listen closely. If you do, you surely can hear it.

You're one, my dear, who has the true gift
of giving to others, of helping to lift
their burdens. You do this just by your caring,
by who you are, by the virtue of sharing.

And I do believe it is truly smart
to share who we are, straight from the heart.
When I think of your life, you're so very busy.
The chores that you carry. It makes me quite dizzy.

Whenever you find you're in need of a chat,
please call – if you can find time for that!

ANONYMOUS

I have a secret sister,
I don't know who she is.
She sends me lovely greetings,
and I can tell you this.

She's thoughtful, loving, caring,
and I cannot wait to see
just who this lady is that's always
sending gifts to me.

Every day when I get up
I must go and look. I stare
as I scroll down to the bottom
to see if she's been there.

Her messages are pure delight.
I so enjoy her greetings,
and one day in near future,
I hope that we'll be meeting.

Having no real-life sister,
it's especially great to see
a loving secret sister
who shows she cares for me.

CIRCLE OF FRIENDS

Our "Circle of Friends" grows ever wider
with every event we attend.
We blossom with red, purple and white,
and often we meet a new friend.

Gathering for fun is what we're about,
and various things we have tried.
A few went zip lining sometime last June.
Oh My God, what a ride!

There's train rides, and bowling
and lunches and teas.
There's shows and there's plays,
and shopping. Yes, Please!

It's great to belong to a wonderful group.
We gather together and share.
We circle our friends when troubles arise,
and they are in need of some care.

Supporting each other through thick
and through thin, is also what we're about.
Yes, "Circle of Friends" is a very good name.
It says who we are without doubt.

REIKI

And how, pray tell, is the way we can grow?
T'is by hearing from others just what they know.
For it's by our experiences, all of us each
can garner the knowledge with which we can teach.

By listening carefully we surely can learn
those facets of life for which we still yearn.
Evolving serenity. We have been hoping
to breathe out compassion, live honest and open.

So we each, in our way, steadily seek
the purpose of life and find ourselves meek,
laying down posture and becoming more real,
and working to change the ways that we feel.

We continue to discover how feelings can cease
when those feelings become the cost of our peace.
Oh Yes! We *can* claim a brand new identity,
as we learn yet more tools to bring us serenity.

The timing was right. We each found the place
where we came together in such sacred space.
We had a need to be there, all of us knew.
From my heart, I am grateful to each one of you!

CHOIR DIRECTOR

Alice, dear Alice, I hear you are going.
Without your direction how will choir be flowing?
There are other directors. I know this is true,
but other directors will **not** be you.
And while it may well be time you must go,
we can wish in our hearts that it wasn't so.

Many has been the long winter night
it was hard to get going. It was a fight.
I wanted to stay home warm in my chair
and not gather up things to get going there.
Had to lecture myself, internal voice strong,
to **not** stay at home 'cuz that would be wrong.

If you can come teach us. Yea, travel miles,
then we can show up with nothing but smiles.
And always I'm glad I made myself show.
Because I left practice feeling a glow.
Your humour, your patience and talent I'm sure,
made practice fun, not a thing to endure.

You made it a place where I could belong
without ever knowing the notes of a song.
And lucky I am, though, that I can hear,
and pick up the sound of the song with my ear.
I thank you for that, and say without guile,
when I think of you, I know I will smile.

LADIES OF THE HEART

I bless the Universe that gave you the heart
to love all of us and play such a part
of our connecting together to share our success,
to affirm ourselves each and to certainly bless.
Others who read and are likewise inspired,
when sharing creativity get even more fired,
who then go on to help others in need,
finding themselves performing good deeds.

Yours is the needle and thread that go through
the connecting and supporting in Tidbits we do.
Not only success, we share hurt and pain.
When we do, we each, yes, all of us gain.
A sharing of burdens by many made lighter,
a tomorrow that miraculously somehow gets brighter,
because we've reached out and been able to share.
We're not alone. There's many that care.

So Bless You, Dear Kari, for yours is a gift
that gives many a burdensome spirit the lift
that comes of our speaking and having thoughts heard,
and sharing the feelings though we speak not a word.
For remember, those who can speak do it now,
and those who are silent are still with you somehow.
It is the praying of many, whether silent or loud
that brings about courage to move through a shroud.

We all help each other. Of this I am sure,
giving love to all is a way we can cure
the hurts in ourselves, and then on the earth,
which greatly needs healing, an awakening birth.
So, whether we do or do not agree,
we accept each other and let everyone be.
For we are **all of us** learning as fast as we can,
each child, each woman, each parent, each man.

VOLUNTEERS

It was the year two thousand and nine
we joined a club that turned out just fine.
We're glad we attended that very first meeting.
Now, at events, new friends we are greeting.
When the Canadian Club started, no one could know
how word would spread, how much it would grow.
The secret is out and folks want to come
to join in a group that has so much fun.

There's bowling, there's bocce and then there are hikes.
On Sunday there's slow pitch. Our ump calls the strikes.
When the gals go to lunch, lounge lizards appear,
and may well consume more than one beer.
In February... a Valentine's Dance,
with costumes and finery worth more than one glance.
Once a month there is potluck with food oh-so-good
that most of us eat much more than we should.
Pickle ball weekly for those into the sport.
Disappointment abounds when they can't get the court.

We go to the Elks for spaghetti or ribs.
They give us good food, but forget to give bibs.
On Fridays the golfers hit l'il balls about.
When they hit a good one, you hear a big shout.
Friendships are formed at the places we go.
We just keep on meeting those we'd like to know.

At every meeting Olga takes minutes.
It has all the information we need in it.
The man who runs meetings - his name is Jim.
Everyone attending appreciates him.
We all know that it's not a rumor.
Each meeting we witness his great sense of humour.
He greets folks by name and we must confess,
how he remembers we cannot guess.

And then there is Deb, dubbed Mother Superior.
She started it all, her goal not ulterior.
She wanted Canadians to gather together
to enjoy each other in all kinds of weather.
When we send info for her to send out,
it shall be done. There is no doubt.
We are all grateful. She deserves praise.
What do you think? Should we give her a raise?

All kidding aside, we appreciate
those who organize, and work hard. But wait.
Now that you've read this poem, here's the rub.
Without volunteers, there'd be no club!

WORK, PLAY

The beds are made, the dishes done.
I'll take my tea and sit in sun.
Enjoy the time I have before
I must get up and do some more.
Letters to write, groceries to buy,
Laundry basket piled high.
Phone calls to make, dinner to start.
See my best friend, have heart to heart.
And yes, it's true, at times I get tired.
There are others when I feel quite inspired.
And when I'm aware, I do rejoice,
because, you see, it's all my choice!

KNOWING YOU

Knowing you, you cannot do less.
how long you can do it is anyone's guess.
You're good to your father, you're good to your son.
Yet with all that, you still are not done.

You're good to your grandchild and good to your man.
You give of yourself as only you can.
And as I watch, I'll tell you this true,
my biggest worry is, who's there for you?

For you to continue this way, I you will tell,
there must be some ways to fill up your well.
'Cuz you're only one and can't do it all.
My worry for you is you'll take a big fall.

NEW FRIEND

You know we'll miss your crazy ass,
and hope you bring it back real fast.
Although we've come to care about'cha,
we'll have to carry on without'cha.

Perhaps you'll move up here one day,
and you will join us when we play
Mexican Train, or some other game.
Without you, it just won't be the same.
In the meantime, God Bless yours and you.
We gonna miss ya through and through.

MOVING

I'm sad you are moving,
yet know you must go,
to where your heart leads,
to allow you to grow.
You will leave me with more
than one pleasant memory.
And when I think of you,
I feel your warm energy.

For me, as for you,
that's as important as air.
It's the essence of us.
It's what we now share
with others we meet
along our life's way.
We feed on good energy.
what more can I say?

As your new life moves along,
you will be met with success.
New horizons are waiting.
Take care. And God Bless!

LAUGHTER

There is a fellow that I know.
His given name is Herb.
Although he's quite intelligent,
he sometimes acts absurd.

That's just his sense of humour.
He fills the room with laughter.
Good feelings that vibrate within,
continue some days after.

Absurdity is lots of fun.
You see, I'm that way, too.
It's just the way we look at things,
and we enjoy the view.

When I spend time at his house,
I always get my kicks.
It's lots of fun, you see, it is.
I get my Herbie fix.

I CAN

I know there's nothing I can do
to take the pain away from you.

I know there's nothing I can say
to make your worries go away.

But I can send you love and light
to help you make it through the night.

And I can think of you and pray,
to help you make it through the day.

My heart and soul just need to be
the kind of friend you've been to me.

REALTOR

Although we looked around a bit, we found it really hard
to find the words we want to say in a Thank-You card.
And so we thought we'd better sit down and write a poem
to thank you for your help in building our new home.

Long before we made the move, you kept us up to date,
so we could see what's happening in Okanagan real estate.
While other realtors told us they would keep in touch,
they didn't follow through. That didn't help us much.

And yet, you didn't pester us, or tell us we should move,
and that, dear John, is something anyone would love.
It must be such a fine line to help... but not too much.
It seems that you have mastered it. You have a gentle touch.

From the very beginning and right up to the end,
we thought not of you as realtor, but more of you as friend.
You have a way of listening to things we had to ask,
and made it seem a pleasure, not merely one more task.

It has really been a pleasure to get the help from you,
and know the answers given would be checked
and would be true.
When we had some questions, you never made us wait.
That is one more trait of yours we do appreciate.

We'd also like to thank you for the lovely gift you brought.
It is unique and beautiful. We like it quite a lot.
Please know that in the future, this is what we'll do,
when someone needs a realtor, we'll send them to you.

WEEKEND

Deb and Stan... or Stan and Deb,
we don't know how to say
how much appreciate
that you invited us to play.
The company, the toys, the food
were plentiful and fun.
Conversation everywhere,
and... did you order sun?

Walking thru' your gardens
of flowers, big and small,
each display delightful.
Where do you find them all?
The private little corners
where one could sit and chat,
or read a book in solitude,
or stroke a silky cat.

Or join a game of quarters
with others of like mind,
or take a stroll around the grounds,
not knowing what we'll find.
Llamas, donkey, cats and dogs
put on quite a show.
Each one, all so precious,
And we love them so.

Good music Stan kept playing,
great tunes old and new,
accompanied by laughter,
as we shared a joke or two.
Then as the night descended,
a roaring fire in the pit
would slowly draw us, one and all.
We'd bring our chairs and sit.

Finally some would drift away
to prepare themselves for bed.
The ones who stayed up latest
would have the biggest head.
And so we thank the pair of you
for everything you've done,
and want the both of you to know
that both of us had fun!

DINNER

Thank you for the visit. Thank you for the meal.
We want you to know exactly how we feel.
There's nothing we can think of that could be a greater gift,
though the time we spent with you went by oh-so-swift.

No sooner did we get there, when it seemed time to go,
Although the time was fleeting, we still want you to know
we appreciate your time and we appreciate your skill.
And we sure loved the shrimp you cooked out there on your grill.

Every bit of the food you served was oh-so-good,
and we savoured every bite, like we knew we would.
Please, do not have worries. And please do not have fear.
We'll come to you for dinner when we return again next year!

NEIGHBOURS

Thanks, our dear friends, for the visit and dinner.
Outings at your place are always a winner.
Always good fun to see everyone.
Always so good to sit in the sun.
We are all blessed to live where we do,
to have connected with others, with each other, too.

There's no other place we'd rather to live,
where we're not just neighbours, but are friends who give
whatever is needed, whatever the time.
If one needed help at midnight, that'd be fine.
We all join together to help one another,
just like we're family – like a sister or a brother.

It's something special we have created.
Each of us moving here seemed to be fated.
We each came to town, we each chose our street,
not knowing how much more 'family' we'd meet.
Now look what has happened. Look what we've done.
We're blessed to be here. And we love everyone.

TRIBUTE ARTIST

How could we ever tell you?
We think you'll have to guess.
There is no way to find the words
that adequately express
the joy you bring into our hearts
when you put on a show.
Use your imagination,
and then perhaps you'll know.

You come and do your Elvis thing
for an older group of ladies.
Some not as old as others,
and some approaching eighties.
And through it all you make us feel
that we are young again.
We all love you, Adam.
But then... we guess that's plain.

TURNING FIFTY

With turning fifty, life just starts,
more sure of self, more sharing hearts.
Gone the adolescent youth.
We're soaring now. And that's the truth.

We spread our wings and learn to fly.
I'm sure we are a mile high.
'Cuz now we know there is no limit.
No boundary stifles us within it.

We know we only have today.
While we must work, we also play.
We've learned a lot from days long past,
to nurture friendships that will last.

To hang onto those who do encourage,
let go of those who will discourage
for reasons only they can know.
We've found out we can let go.

We fill our days with other things,
with fun and joy that knowing brings.
Surround ourselves with joy and fun,
relax for hours in the sun.

We do what our hearts desire,
setting this 'ole world on fire.
Fifty years is now thought young,
at least for those of us among

those that go about and do.
Kim, you're one of those folks, too.
I tip my hat to you, my friend,
in love and friendship without end.

NEW DOCTOR

When we already have a doctor
it is difficult to find
another one who'll take us on.
It puts us in a bind.

What if the doctor that we have
isn't helping us at all?
What is it then that we can do
to get one on the ball?

When I came in to ask for help,
I was hanging by a thread.
I couldn't sleep, yet when awake
all I felt was dread.

Constant pain excruciating,
"Help me, please." I said.
Can't live like this much longer.
I wished that I was dead.

I came to you with heart in hand.
You saw my desperation.
Not looking for a miracle,
just some pain cessation.

I feel so very, very blessed.
You told me what to do.
My hubby needs to bring me in.
Finally, a clue.

Dr. E. might take me.
His list grows ever longer.
Lucky us, 'cuz when he does.
Our health can get much stronger.

He listened to my symptoms.
Took copies of my notes.
He figured out the problem.
Oh **YES!** He has our votes.

We know he can't help everyone.
Too bad. That's a sin.
Maybe we can clone him?
And everyone can win.

THE DAY WE WED

I remember well the day we wed.
The precious vows that we both said,
today remain all ever true,
the loving vows I took with you.

Impossible, the time that's passed.
Endearing how our love has last.
Cannot envision one whole minute
living life without you in it.

Children grown and gone away,
no longer do they fill our day.
Truer now than was before,
together facing life's long shore.

Happenings, both good and bad,
life's events, most gay, some sad.
I'm glad that love has passed the test
of time. Our marriage has been blessed.

WEDDING DAY

Today is the wondrous day you will wed.
You will always remember the words that you said.
We all saw the happiness, evinced by the tears,
as you both look ahead to the wonderful years
you'll share together, as man and as wife,
enjoying the ways you can plan out your life.

There is so much to do and so much to see.
I wish you success, wherever you be.
And as your love deepens with time, it is true
there will be many good things happening for you.
Today and forever, I wish you, my friends,
a life path of happiness and health without end.

UNITED

Sweet Julie, I've known you most of my life.
I'm overjoyed you've said you'll be my wife.
I've seen you happy and I've seen you in pain.
I've seen you work hard, and I've seen you gain
a spirit that spreads joy wherever it goes,
with sunshine and love. Everyone knows.
Your quiet strength will bless us indeed
when we hit troubled waters and feel the need.

Dear Chad, you have been the love of my life,
and I will be honoured to be your wife.
I've witnessed your courage. I've seen how you strive
to do your best always. I see how you thrive
on working with children in the name of the Lord.
Doing God's work, we are both in accord.
We believe in each other, believe in the way.
I value your spirit. What else can I say?

Together, united, we cannot go wrong,
for now we are bonded and are twice as strong.
We fit together like a hand in a glove,
and both thank the Lord for our wonderful love.

LISTEN *AND* HEAR

As you, in your glory, and you, in your youth,
become man and wife, always walk in your truth.
For just as your new life today has begun,
you now are not two, in God's eyes, but one.

As you change in your life and walk your new walk,
don't only listen, but hear each of you talk.
For if you can't hear, you won't understand
why the other is different sometimes. This is planned

by God and the Universe. By hearing, we learn
to sometimes make change. And change, it can turn
the dark into light, when dark's all we know,
and we need light to guide us, help us to grow.

Even when happy, things can go wrong.
With love and support of each other, we're strong.
Truth is, "United we Stand. Divided we Fall."
As Christians you have both heard the Lord's call.

As you are His children, you're now wife and man.
Walk in God. Love each other. This is surely God's plan.
Be good to each other. Treat each other like gold.
A precious gift, love, you've been given to hold.

ADVICE

Brendan and Laura, here's sage advice
you may want to read more than twice.
Brendan, if you want to avoid a fight,
you must remember, Laura is right.
Women are different. They need tender touch.
Men don't always understand this so much.
And Laura, here is a much different spin –
every once in awhile, just let him win!

You both know I am funning with you.
You two alone will decide what to do.
Not staying locked in who's right or who's wrong
will definitely help your marriage stay strong.
Relationships are hard. We all have our ways.
They go oh-so-much smoother when we remember to praise
our partner for the little things that they do.
It feels awesome to them. It feels good to you, too.

You build up a love bank from which to withdraw
without wasting time to let anger thaw.
Benefits are many. What does it cost
to give in with grace? All is not lost.
No need to feel anger. No need to feel sorrows.
Living with love leads to happy tomorrows.

SIXTY YEARS

As the two of you walk down the memory lane
of your marriage of sixty years,
you'll no doubt remember the laughter.
You'll no doubt remember the tears.

For life is full of surprises
that we all must take in stride.
The roller-coaster of ups and downs
you've ridden side-by-side.

The welcoming that Peg received
from George's dog, named 'Zip'.
On their wedding day, from Peggy's dress,
that canine took a nip.

Soon George was in the Army
and called away to war,
facing uncertainties of life and death,
they knew not what's in store.

From mechanic to Husky bulk oil sales,
to the water treatment plant,
and always in a hurry,
with no such word as can't.

No matter what got broken,
George would have to fix.
The 'Mr. Fix-It' nickname
is a name for him that sticks.

While George was off and fighting,
Peg did what she could,
helping wherever needed,
unselfishly doing good.

And when the war was over,
Peg always did her part,
raising the kids while holding down jobs.
Oh yes, this gal has heart.
Cooking, baking and knitting,
her love of plants and flowers,
have given their family much pleasure,
as they congregate for hours.

Visiting, enjoying, reliving the past
with relatives from out of town,
who gather together at their place.
Hearty welcomes they've always been shown.

During your lives you've seen several firsts,
radio, television and phone,
electronic technology, computers and such
have become commonplace in the home.

You've both seen peace. You've both seen war.
You've seen man's ascent into space.
You've no doubt occasionally questioned
the state of the human race.

And when your children have needed you,
you've always lent a hand.
No matter what the issue has been,
you've tried to understand.

Your pride in your grandchildren
is obvious to all.
You've loved them and been there for them
from the time that they were small.

Congrats from all who know you,
each of us wishes you well,
and hope your anniversary celebration
will in every way be swell.

OUR LAND

God I love this country. God I love this land.
I would have loved to be alive
when this whole thing was planned.

Were all trees given numbers
like every hair on our head?
And if wasn't trees He planted
What would He have planted instead?

Would we have mega flowers
reaching right up to the sky?
Would there still be weeds... or nothing?
Now there's a thought. Oh my!

Nothing in this land of ours,
just one big abyss.
But if we knew not better,
then nothing we would miss.

I'm glad He planned the way He did.
Air, water, fire, on earth.
Let's enjoy whatever we see.
And be thankful for our birth.

WILD FLOWER

Oh wild flower, so sweet, so true.
What gift to me does come from you?
As I walk, on you I gaze.
Your beauty doth my sense engage.

Who planted you? From where the seed?
My spirits lift. That's what I need.
Walking lone on dyke's old soil,
my head, emotions in turmoil.

Thinking this and that with feeling,
leaving mind and spirit reeling.
Imagined slights with things unsaid,
plug up my mind, and fill my head.

And then I see your beauty rare,
erasing turmoil, losing care.
Just drinking in each inch of you,
and seeing world through eyes now new.

Dreadful thoughts have gone away.
Oh how you've brightened up my day.
So often passed, not really seen,
when you give so much, a mind serene.

BEAUTY

In our garden, a yellow rose that surprisingly survives
the frosts and snows of winter. Not only lives. It thrives
through most the winter season, ten days away from spring.
Witnessing it's courage has caused my heart to sing.
That yellow rose brought joy to me. I carried joy each day.
I cheered and loved that little rose and hoped that it could stay.
One night a cold deep frost came in... It died.
I saw the death of beauty, and I admit I cried.
Sad because it's gone now, but joyful it did live,
reminding me that all of us have gifts that we can give.

THINGS I'VE LOST

My purse and my camera,
my socks and my shoes.
I wonder how many more
things I can lose.
Try to be diligent, put them away.
When I look they are gone,
to where, I can't say.
There's a place for my keys,
and a place for my sweater,
all gone. Yup. They're gone
I hope it gets better.
I look for my glasses,
only to find
they're up on the head,
which should house my mind.
My mind has been missing.
They call it brain fog.
I don't have the thinking
that God gave a dog.
I forget what I'm doing,
I forget who I am,
though with non-remembering,
I don't give a damn.
But in days of more clearness,
in days of good thinking,
I'm aware there are times
when my thinking is stinking.

DRESSING UP

Dressing up is so much fun,
no matter what our age.
To don our finest finery
all our senses doth engage.

Picking out the fancy clothes,
or borrowing a dress,
as we harbour imaginations,
of how we'll look, no less.

Going to the beauty shop
to get a hair-do done,
makes us feel so special
and is a lot of fun.

Next, we really must make sure
nails are polished to a T,
"Ladies hands are important."
my mother said to me.

The time is drawing nearer,
as we slip into our dress.
We anticipate with butterflies,
sure the night will bless.

We pack our cocktail purses,
and put our nylons on.
It's almost time. We're ready,
and we will soon be gone.

And then out comes the camera,
as we strike up a pose,
carried along by excitement,
and feeling like a rose.

Laughter is what greets us
when we walk through the door.
All the ladies sharing.
Gosh. Who could ask for more?

We 'oooooh' and 'aaaaah' o'er all the clothes
the other ladies wear.
We look gorgeous in our finery,
like queens, each one, I swear.

We chat, we eat, we socialize.
The night does pass quite swiftly.
Before we know it, time to leave,
the evening was... well... nifty.

Home again, with pleasured hearts,
and much to our chagrin,
we find the best part of dressing up
is getting undressed again!!

PERCEPTIONS

When I was only three-years-old,
and jumped off of the stair,
it seems to last forever
that I stayed up in the air.

And that old tree we played in,
I climbed it to the sky.
Through three-year-old eyes, I'm sure
I must have climbed a mile high.

I couldn't fathom distance,
and felt so very strong
when I jumped across the puddle
that was half a mile long.

And jumping from those back stairs?
Oh! I was so impressed.
How I could manage such a feat
is anybody's guess.

Then, when I was older,
and visited that place,
and saw it all through adult eyes,
how tiny is that space.

How short the jump from second step
I used to think so great.
As I waited for my turn to jump,
my heart was in a state.

Reality had struck me dumb.
I couldn't get it through my head,
that what I saw was not what is,
but was much different instead.

Perhaps when I was three-years old
I wasn't very wise.
But oh! I love the distances
I saw through younger eyes.

PASS IT ON

To all those folks who saw something in me...
They saw something valuable that I couldn't see.
They saw brains and they also saw humour and guts.
While all I could see made me feel like a klutz.

Therapists, family, a doctor or two,
friends, teachers, preachers, to name just a few.
These people have told me that I have great worth,
while I often wondered what I'm doing on earth.

The long road I chose has been chock-full of difficulties.
I will not deny there's been some atrocities.
And here's the thing that is now different for me,
although it took years for my blind eyes to see.

When I got it, understood I have a choice,
that's when I learned to use my own voice.
When we decide we're responsible for us,
we no longer feel we've been thrown under the bus.

And once we learn this new way to think,
we no longer feel that we're on the brink
of sanity, where life just is not worth living.
We understand we **must** do more giving.

Do unto others what's been done unto me.
Lift them up, care for them and please help them see
that they have great beauty. They have something to give.
And once tried, they'll see it's the best way to live.

We cannot give happiness without getting some, too.
It's just true for me. And it's sure true for you.
And when I go out, when I walk my last mile,
I'll be so proud of me that I'll leave with a smile.

KNOW

All I know is what I know.
But I want to know more. And so
I listen carefully to you.
I know that you can teach me, too.

We, each of us, teach and learn.
To understand yet more I yearn.
And so I listen and I read,
the information that I need

to become a better, gentler me,
to be the best that I can be.
And this work will never end.
This is also true for you, my friend.

TIME MARCHES ON

Time marches on,
doesn't wait for any man,
runs away like lightning.
Catch it if you can.

One day you're a youngster
with your whole life up ahead.
Another day you realize
it's hard to rise from bed.

What happened to the years between
is something we all wonder.
Before we know it, they are gone,
disappeared, asunder.

The best thing we can do for us,
the world, and all that's in it
is realize the gift of time,
and live life every minute.

NO MYSTERY

About who we are, there is no mystery.
We're all about our total history.
So listen close, 'cuz here's the key.
We **are** what we hear, feel, touch and see.
And here's the thing that I have found,
each event in life is wound
into the fabric of our being
and believing so is truly seeing,
rather than the other way.
What is the saying that they say?
They say, "Seeing is Believing."
That's not at all what I'm perceiving.
I think the opposite is true.
What is it you think for you?

LIFE'S ROAD

As we walk along life's road,
we meet those that surely teach,
who gently support and show us
what we thought was out of reach.
And while we struggle, learning,
sometimes we forget,
that while we learn from others,
from us they also get
ways of seeing through our eyes,
things that they've not seen,
a chance to view life differently
from places they have been.

It is our very openness
that allows our souls to grow,
to share love and compassion,
for others that we know.
Those who share themselves with us,
show what's behind the mask,
with whom we then can share ourselves.
This is what we ask.
And once we learn the beauty
of feeling truly free,
to choose in life what's good for us,
it's the way we need to be.

And those of us who did not know,
felt damaged to the core,
must walk awhile and talk awhile
with those who know there's more.
There's more to life than giving up,
surviving day-to-day,
crawling into darkened cave.
Yes! There's another way.

I thank you, Anne, for being there
to support me in my growth.
You shared with me, and cared with me,
and have helped me learn my worth.

PEOPLE

There are people in this world
who think power and control
is where it's at, the place to be.
They believe it is their role.
And it never feels good,
to those who are aware
that manipulation's happening.
But they don't really care.

Do you think they even know
they control at any cost?
Doesn't matter if it's fair,
or friendships that are lost.
This raging, driving need of theirs,
like a river in a flood,
froths and swells and grows and grows
and leaves a trail of mud.

Better yet to share ourselves
in kind and loving ways,
give care and understanding
to brighten others' days.
I won't try to stand above
and look at you below.
We will stand side by side.
It's the best way that I know.

ME

When I was young, I didn't have a worry, thought, or care.
I didn't think that I would age. And I thought life was fair.

In the wisdom wrought by time, I see things differently.
Oh! That I'd known what I now know, I'd be a different me.

And time, it has the strangest way of turning hair to grey.
Speeding like a bullet, the past becomes today.

And if I'd known the future? Would I really want to change
the past into the future? Would my life I rearrange?

The way my life unfolded? What would I want to be?
No matter what, if I did that, I would not be me.

TOGETHER

Together weeds and flowers grow
without a struggle, 'cuz they don't know,
they're different, and should **not** co-exist.
Now, isn't that a funny twist?

We humans are **much** more advanced,
and differentness must **not** be chanced.
For if we're different and don't agree,
then one is wrong. And it can't be me.

I must convince you at all cost,
or pride and dignity will be lost.
I'm right. You're wrong. You're wrong. I'm right.
'Til one gives in to end the fight.

You **never** see the plant life fight.
They seem to know that they're alright.
And when a flower is choked away,
it sows its seeds another day.

One hopes one day we'll look around
and heed the lessons that abound
in nature, in all living things,
and feel the peace that **knowing** brings.

ALONE, NOT LONELY

Amidst fifty years of living in other folk's clutter,
I need to have time alone, she would mutter.
I need to spend some time in a place
where there's only me and myself in my space.
Time to reflect, and time to decide
the things I can, and cannot abide.
Time to look at the flowers and trees
and smell the soft, billowy freshness of breeze.
Time to plan future, the years that remain
in ways that make me feel good and feel sane.

Time spent alone, I find very well spent.
Others demands on me I resent.
Their needs are too needy, and they cannot see
how their expectations drain the life out of me.
They cannot help but need what they need.
And I silently watch the blood from me bleed.
I don't want to change them. I want to be where
I connect with those who can hear and who care.
Who try understanding what I am about,
instead of turning me inside and out
to be what it is they want me to be.
That surely spells death and destruction to me.

It does not mean that either are wrong,
when we get to the place where we can't get along.
We each have our feelings. On that we agree.
But it seems to hurt **you** when I express me.
And it hurts **me** when I don't express.
I can't see a way out of this mess.
I love time alone. I get to be me.
It makes me feel good, and it makes me feel free.
I don't have to worry how others may act,
or how they make statements, that, to them are a fact.
Where one needs to be either wrong or be right,
and to make me agree is a reason to fight.

I will nourish my spirit. I will take my rest.
I'll connect with my friends, and I won't feel so stressed.
There are those who support me, who truly can hear,
who accept, and reflect who I am in a mirror.
They show me my beauty, reflecting my soul,
and I come away always feeling quite whole,
not torn apart, and less than I was
when I am made wrong and called names because
I have said something about how I feel,
where again and again I am battered by steel.
I know what feels good and I know what feels not,
and I don't need to stay in a place where I'm caught,
in a place where I really do not want to be.
'Cuz there's love and acceptance waiting for me.

WRITING GROUP

When I joined other writers, I couldn't have guessed
that I'd come away so very impressed.
When I read their stories, I feel inspired.
My mind, heart and soul all get really wired.
To get words onto paper. Indeed. Use my voice,
that I've now learned to use, knowing I have the choice
to write what I will, what's been locked up inside,
letting mind, heart and fingers be the true guide.

We all have a story. Of this I am sure.
Getting words onto paper has greatest allure
to many of us with desire to write.
Supporting each other serves to excite
the desire to keep moving, to type up a story,
hand it in for critiquing, with nary a worry
about whether it's good or whether it's bad,
as long as I've given it all that I had.

Getting feedback from others is a way to improve
sentence structure, and such, and we can remove
the parts most redundant, while keeping the rest,
knowing some improvements will be for the best.
It is interesting to me, in reviewing critiquing
there are multiple feedbacks and ways of speaking.
Parts some think need changing, others applaud.
So what is good writing? What is it that's flawed?

Some critiques are one's preference, most do agree,
and I get to decide if the change is for me.
Encouragement rampant. While meeting to share,
we get to read stories written with flair.
They give of their thoughts. They give of their time.
In thinking all that, I've come up with this rhyme.
Not all groups are so welcoming as this seems to be,
and I thank all of you for welcoming me.

MY ANGELS

When 'ere I call my angels, they fly down from heaven
to surround me with their love. There is always seven.
I see the detail of their wings, each and every feather.
They circle to protect me, standing all together.

A white peace settles over me as I drink in their love.
I **always** feel the comfort they bring me from above.
In gentle peace, my heart sings, while cares all drift away.
I'd love to keep them with me, but, alas, they cannot stay.

They only come to comfort me, and when that's done, they fly,
returning to celestial home way up in the sky.
And I? Oh yes, I miss them and wish they'd stay with me,
but they, like all of us, have their home, and it simply cannot be.

And so, I bless their coming, and know that they must go,
am grateful for their presence, and they'll be back, I know.

IT ALL COMES BACK

Anything given comes back to you.
He gives. I give. I know that it's true.
When you're with someone who knows how to give,
it's a wondrously, happy way you can live.

I finally learned how to listen and heed
the feelings that tell me what I really need.
When I know my own worth and accept nothing less,
than full love and good treatment, I have been blessed.

Tenderness given returns hundredfold.
Love given away brings back all you can hold.
The love in our hearts cannot be depleted,
but expands and expands, never defeated.

This holds true for lover and friend.
We tend to get everything back that we send.
Good, bad, indifferent. It's up to us each.
if we want acceptance, then we have to teach.

You'll know the peace that living well brings.
And know, too, that love is life's finest thing.
Can't be taken or forced, or driven from you.
It may hide awhile – but comes shining through

when awakened by those who return it so well.
You will know who they are. You surely can tell
those who love you for you, and not how you look,
those who know the cover does not make the book.

So don't be afraid to hold out your hand.
Try not to be fearful of taking a stand.
For you will attract those, who, like you, truly care
and give real acceptance, if only you dare.

CELEBRATE

I celebrate disconnection with all that feels toxic.
I celebrate selection of all that feels good.
I do not spend time where I am not seen.
There was a time I didn't know that I could.

I change things around me within my power.
I let go of things I cannot control.
It is treasured gift to have found this pathway.
The ways I think now, satisfy soul.

Amazing, just amazing, the light shining within,
now ghosts of the past have been put to rest.
Life full of joy, the future is cherished.
Within I now celebrate how I've been blessed.

ABOUT THE AUTHOR

Lin Brian is a life-long lover of poetry. Over her 30 years as a writer, her work has been published in a plethora of volumes, including newspapers, newsletters, brochures, and programs. Her poems are featured in the *Okanagan Tapestry*, an anthology of Penticton, British Columbia Writers, in *Offerings from the Oasis*, Volume 8, an anthology of the Lake Havasu City, Arizona Writer's Group, in Joseph Seiler's true story, *Out of Paralysis,* in Paul L. Bailey's novella, *The Rich Boys,* and in The Gottman Institute publications.

Lin has been contracted to write, and has fun writing specific poems about specific people. A number of them are in this book. In addition, she has recently delved into the Murder Mystery genre, to be included in a book Easytime Publishing hopes to release soon.

This, Lin Brian's second book of poetry, will be followed by one more. Her third book will feature introspective poems selected from Lin's collection, while several other poems will be developed into children's books.

Writing continues to call her, and at times, it's too loud to ignore.

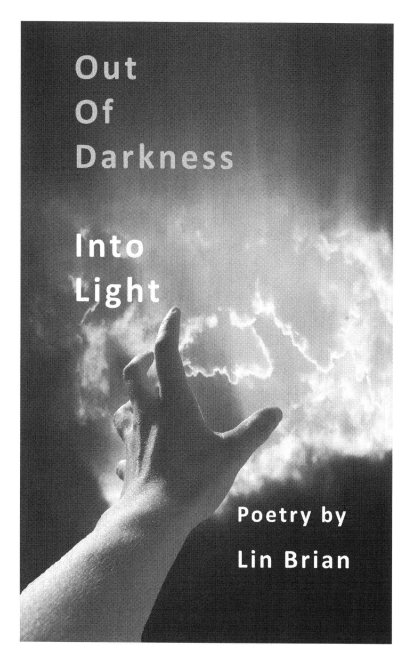

Experience the life-changing poetry of Lin Brian
Get her first book, "Out of Darkness Into Light"
Available from Amazon.com and from EasytimePublishing.com

Made in the USA
San Bernardino, CA
26 January 2018